KT-485-737

HOME BAKING
RECIPES

Breads, Buns & Teacakes

compiled by
Carol Wilson

SALMON

Index

Cover *front:* Dinner Time *by Arthur H. Davies* *back:* The Cornfield (detail) *by John Constable*
Title page: The Finished Loaves *by Hellen Allingham*

Printed and Published by J. Salmon Ltd., Sevenoaks, England © Copyright

Barley Bread

Barley was once widely used in baking but is rarely used nowadays. It makes bread with a distinctive flavour. Barley meal can be bought in Health Food shops..

1½ oz fresh yeast   **2 teaspoons salt**
10-12 fl oz warm water   **1 lb barley meal**

Crumble the yeast into 5 fl oz warm water and leave until frothy (about 5 minutes). Stir the salt into the rest of the water. Put the barley meal into a large mixing bowl and make a well in the centre. Pour in the yeast mixture followed by the salted water and mix well to form a dough. Turn out on to a floured surface and knead well for 10 minutes until smooth. Return to the bowl and cover with a clean tea towel. Leave in a warm place to rise until doubled in size. Turn out on to a floured surface and knock back to remove the air. Shape into a round and place on a greased baking sheet. Cover and leave to prove for 20 to 30 minutes until risen. Meanwhile, set oven to 450°F or Mark 8 and then bake for 30 to 40 minutes. Tap the bottom of the loaf and if it sounds hollow it is cooked. If not, return to the oven for another 5 minutes. Cool on a wire rack.

A Highland Cottage *by Birket Foster*

Baps

First recorded in a Scottish text in the sixteenth century, the origin of the name of these soft flat rolls is unknown.

1 lb strong white flour	**2 teaspoons granulated sugar**
1 teaspoon salt	**1 oz fresh yeast**
2 oz lard	**10 fl oz warm milk and water, mixed**

Sift the flour and salt into a large mixing bowl and rub in the fat until the mixture resembles breadcrumbs. Add half the sugar. Cream the yeast with the remaining sugar and add to the warm liquid. Leave until frothy; about 5 minutes. Pour the liquid into the flour and work to a soft dough. Turn out on to a floured surface and knead until smooth and elastic. Place in a lightly oiled bowl, cover with a clean tea towel and leave to rise in a warm place for 1 hour. Knead the dough again and divide into 10 pieces. Shape into rounds and place on a greased baking sheet. Cover with a clean tea towel and leave in a warm place to prove for 20 minutes. Meanwhile, set oven to 450°F or Mark 8. Sprinkle each bap with a little flour and bake for 20 minutes. Wrap in a clean tea towel to keep the baps soft as they cool.

Lincolnshire Plum Loaf

In the past dried prunes were used in fruitcakes and breads and thus these became known as 'plum cake or bread'. Nowadays, although prunes almost never feature in such recipes, the term 'plum' is still used and denotes dried fruits.

1 lb strong white flour	**8 oz dried fruits**
Pinch of salt	**(raisins, currants, etc.)**
1 oz fresh yeast	**1 oz candied peel, chopped**
8 oz butter	**1 egg, beaten**
8 oz granulated sugar	**1 teaspoon bicarbonate of soda**

5 fl oz warm milk

Set oven to 350°F or Mark 4. Grease and line a 2 lb loaf tin. Sift the flour and salt into a large mixing bowl and rub in the yeast. Rub in the butter until the mixture resembles fine breadcrumbs, then stir in the sugar, dried fruits and peel. Work the egg into the mixture. Dissolve the bicarbonate of soda in the warm milk and pour into the mixture. Mix well and put into the tin. Bake for 1½ hours. Cool on a wire rack.

Fruited Tea Bread

*Use any fruit tea, for example Orange, Apple & Ginger, Rosehip & Hibiscus,
to impart an intriguing flavour.*

1 lb mixed dried fruit	**2 tablespoons marmalade**
8 oz Demerara sugar	**1 teaspoon ground cinnamon**
Warm tea of your choice	**1 egg**
1 lb self-raising flour	

Put the fruit and sugar into a large bowl and just cover with warm tea. Cover and leave overnight. Next day, set oven to 325ºF or Mark 3 and grease and base line a 2 lb loaf tin. Stir the marmalade, cinnamon, egg and flour into the soaked fruit and beat well until thoroughly combined. Spoon into the tin and bake for about 90 minutes until a skewer inserted comes out clean. Leave in the tin for 15 minutes before turning out on to a wire rack to cool. Store in an airtight tin for 24 hours before cutting. Serve sliced, spread with butter.

Revel Buns

These golden yellow buns which are similar to the Cornish Saffron Cake, were made in the West Country for the Whitsun festivities or revels, held on Whit Sunday and Whit Monday.

½ teaspoon saffron strands	2 oz butter
3 tablespoons warm milk	2 oz currants
8 oz flour	1 oz fresh yeast
Pinch of salt	1 teaspoon caster sugar
½ teaspoon ground cinnamon	2 oz thick double or clotted cream

1 beaten egg to glaze

Stir the saffron into the warm milk, cover and leave to stand overnight. Next day, sift the flour, salt and cinnamon into a mixing bowl and rub in the butter. Add the currants and make a well in the centre. Reheat the saffron milk until warm but not hot. Cream the yeast and sugar and leave for a few minutes until frothy, then gradually add the saffron milk, including the saffron strands, the cream and almost all the egg. Pour into the well and mix to a soft dough. Turn out on to a floured surface and knead for 2 to 3 minutes. Return to the bowl, cover with a clean tea towel and leave in a warm place until doubled in size. Divide into 8 pieces and shape each into a round bun. Place on a greased baking sheet, cover and leave in a warm place for 20 minutes. Meanwhile, set oven to 375°F or Mark 5. Brush lightly with the beaten egg and bake for 15 to 20 minutes until golden brown. Cool on a wire rack.

Fowey, Cornwall *by E.W. Haslehust*

Cattern Cakes

St. Catherine was the patron saint of lace makers who celebrated the saint's feast day on November 25th by serving these delectable little cakes which were named after her.

9 oz self-raising flour	**2 oz ground almonds**
¼ teaspoon ground mixed spice	**7 oz granulated sugar**
Pinch of cinnamon	**4 oz butter, melted**
2 oz currants	**1 egg, beaten**

Granulated sugar and cinnamon for sprinkling

Set oven to 400°F or Mark 6. Grease a baking tray. Sift the flour and spices into a mixing bowl and stir in the currants, ground almonds and sugar. Add the melted butter and the egg and mix to a soft dough. Roll out on a floured surface to a rectangle about 12 x 10 inches. Brush the dough with water and sprinkle with the extra sugar and cinnamon. Roll up like a Swiss roll and cut into slices about ¾ inch thick. Place these well apart on the baking tray and bake for 10 to 15 minutes until cooked. Cool on a wire rack.

Cheese and Onion Bread

A delicious, savoury bread best served warm with soup.

1 medium onion, skinned and diced
1 oz butter
1 lb strong white flour
1 level teaspoon salt

1 level teaspoon dry mustard powder
6 oz Cheddar cheese, grated
½ oz fresh yeast
½ pt tepid water

Set oven to 375°F or Mark 5. Grease two 1 lb loaf tins. Cook the onion in the butter until soft and transparent. Put the flour, salt, mustard and three-quarters of the cheese into a large bowl. Add a little of the tepid water to the yeast to make a smooth cream. Make a well in the dry ingredients and add the yeast liquid, the onion and enough of the remaining water to make a soft, but not sticky dough. Turn on to a floured surface and knead well until the dough is elastic. Cover with a clean tea towel and leave to rise in a warm place until doubled in size. Knead again and divide in two. Place in the tins and leave in a warm place until dough reaches the top. Sprinkle with the remaining cheese and cook for 35 to 45 minutes until golden brown and shrunk slightly from sides of the tin. Turn out to cool on a wire rack.

A Kentish Farm *by C. Essenhigh Corke*

Kentish Huffkins

*These can be eaten plain as bread rolls or the hole in the centre filled with fruit
or jam and topped with whipped cream.*

1 lb strong white flour	1 teaspoon salt
2 oz lard	½ oz fresh yeast
2 teaspoons sugar	½ pt milk and water mixed

Sieve the flour into a warm bowl. Rub the lard into the flour and add the salt and
the sugar. Leave in a warm place for a few minutes. Heat the milk/water until tepid;
crumble the fresh yeast into the liquid and stir until blended. Add the yeast mixture
to the dry ingredients and mix well. Turn out on to a floured surface and knead
until smooth. Return to the bowl, cover with a clean tea towel and leave in a warm
place until doubled in size (about 1 hour). Divide the dough into 12 pieces. Roll
into round balls and place on a greased, floured baking sheet, leaving room
between the rolls for expansion. Press a floured finger into the centre of each roll
to form a hole. Leave in the warm to rise for 20 minutes. Meanwhile, set oven to
425°F or Mark 7 and bake for 20 minutes until risen and golden brown.

Flowerpot Loaves

Grease new clay flowerpots well with lard or oil and bake empty, in a hot oven 400°F or Mark 6 for 30 minutes before use, to avoid cracking later.

8 oz strong wholemeal flour	1 teaspoon caster sugar
6 oz strong white flour	10 fl oz warm water
2 teaspoons salt	1 tablespoon chopped fresh herbs (optional)
1 oz lard	Beaten egg to glaze
1½ oz fresh yeast	Fennel seeds (optional)

Put the flours and salt into a large mixing bowl and rub in the lard. Cream the yeast with the sugar and add the water, mixing well. Pour into the flour mixture and mix to a soft dough. Add the fresh herbs at this stage, if using. Turn out on to a floured surface and knead until smooth, shape into a ball and return to the bowl. Cover with a clean tea towel and leave to rise for about 1 hour until doubled in size. Knead the dough again and divide into 2 pieces. Place each piece into a well greased flowerpot. Cover and leave to prove for 30 to 40 minutes until risen. Brush the tops with beaten egg and sprinkle with fennel seeds if using. Meanwhile, set oven to 400°F or Mark 6. Stand the pots on a baking sheet and bake for about 35 minutes. When cooked the loaves will sound hollow when turned out and tapped on the base. If not, return to the oven for another 5 minutes. Turn out carefully on to a wire rack to cool.

Oven Bottom Cake

*In Yorkshire this was made with surplus bread dough and was eaten hot
with butter and/or jam.*

1½ lb strong white flour	**2½ teaspoons granulated sugar**
2 teaspoons salt	**15 fl oz warm water**
½ oz fresh yeast	**4 oz lard or butter, diced**

Cream the yeast with the sugar and a little of the warm water and leave to stand until frothy. Sift the flour and salt into a large mixing bowl and pour in the yeast mixture and the remaining water. Mix to a smooth dough and turn out on to a floured surface. Knead until smooth and elastic, then put into a lightly oiled bowl, cover with a clean tea towel and leave in a warm place to rise until doubled in size. Knock back the dough and knead lightly for 2 to 3 minutes. Next, knead the diced fat into the dough, pressing with the knuckles. The dough will be lumpy. Press out into a round and place on a greased baking sheet. Cover and leave to prove until risen. Meanwhile, set oven to 425°F or Mark 7. Bake for 10 minutes then reduce the heat to 375°F or Mark 5 and bake for another 35 minutes. Cool on a wire rack.

Muffins

These are an old fashioned, winter tea time treat, redolent of frosty days and log fires.
Try them toasted and buttered as usual and then, as a variant, topped with ham or cheese.

1 lb strong white flour   **12-14 fl oz warm milk**
1½ teaspoons salt   **½ teaspoon caster sugar**
½ oz fresh yeast   **1 tablespoon melted butter**
Flour for dusting

Sift the flour and salt into a large mixing bowl and make a well in the centre. Cream the yeast with 5 fl oz warm milk and the sugar until liquid, then add the rest of the milk and the butter. Pour the mixture into the well and beat for a few minutes until a soft, smooth and elastic dough forms. Return to the bowl, cover with a clean tea towel and leave to rise in a warm place until doubled in size. Turn out on to a floured surface and knock back. Roll out to about ½ inch thickness and cut into 9 rounds with a 3 inch plain cutter. Dust with flour and place on a greased baking sheet. Cover and leave to rise in a warm place for 20 to 30 minutes. When risen, cook in batches on a lightly greased hot griddle or heavy frying pan. Cook slowly for about 7 minutes on each side until golden brown. Cool on a wire rack. Split in half, toast, spread with butter and eat hot.

"When Dick the shepherd blows his nail" *by Paul Bertram*

Iced Buns

If preferred, the icing can be coloured pink with a few drops of food colouring.

4 oz butter   **5 fl oz warm milk**   **1 egg**
1 lb strong white flour   **1 oz caster sugar**
Large pinch of salt   **1 oz fresh yeast**
6 oz icing sugar and 1 tablespoon water for icing

Melt the butter, then whisk into the warm milk with the egg. Crumble the yeast into half the milk mixture. Sift the flour into a large mixing bowl and add the sugar and salt. Make a well in the centre and pour in the yeast mixture and the milk mixture. Mix to a soft dough. If too stiff add a little more warm milk. Turn out on to a floured surface and knead until smooth and elastic. Put into a lightly oiled bowl, cover with a clean tea towel and leave in a warm place to rise until doubled in size. Knock back the dough and knead lightly. Roll out on a floured surface to about ½ inch thickness and divide into 12 pieces. Shape into finger length buns and place on a greased baking tray. Cover and leave to prove for 30 minutes until light and puffy. Meanwhile, set oven to 450ºF or Mark 8. Bake for about 20 minutes until light golden brown. Cool on a wire rack, then ice the buns when cold. To make the icing; put the icing sugar and water into a small pan and stir over a very low heat until blended. Quickly pour over the tops of the buns.

Malt Loaf

*This fruity teabread is very easy to make and uses Ovaltine to give
it its distinctive, malty flavour.*

12 oz self-raising flour　**8 oz granulated sugar**
Pinch of salt　**6 oz mixed dried fruit**
3 tablespoons Ovaltine　**½ pt milk**

Set oven to 325°F or Mark 3. Grease and line a 2 lb loaf tin. Sieve the flour and salt
into a mixing bowl, add all the remaining dry ingredients and mix together
thoroughly with the milk. Put into the tin and bake for about 1½ hours or until a
skewer inserted comes out clean. Cover with kitchen foil if the top appears to be
browning too quickly. Turn out on to a wire rack to cool. Serve sliced with butter.

An Old Irish Cabin *by Francis S. Walker*

Irish Treacle Loaf

Black treacle is a popular flavouring for tea loaves and scones in Ireland and this loaf also contains both dried fruit and spice.

2 oz butter	**½ lb flour**
2½ fl oz water	**½ teaspoon ground ginger**
2 oz black treacle	**½ teaspoon ground mixed spice**
2 oz soft brown sugar	**1 teaspoon bicarbonate of soda**
1 egg, beaten	**2 oz currants**

2 oz raisins or sultanas

Set oven to 350°F or Mark 4. Grease and base line one 2 lb or two 1 lb loaf tins. In a pan, melt the butter in the water. Mix together in a bowl the treacle, sugar and beaten egg. Sift together the flour, ginger, spice and bicarbonate of soda and add to the treacle mixture. Fold in the dried fruit and mix thoroughly, then stir in the butter and water mixture. Turn into the tin(s) and bake for 1½ to 2 hours, covering the top with kitchen foil if it appears to be browning too quickly. Allow to cool in the tin(s) for 5 minutes, then turn out on to a wire rack. Serve sliced, plain or with butter.

London Buns

An old recipe for delicious buns that are seldom seen nowadays.

1 lb strong white flour	2 oz butter, melted
2 teaspoons salt	4 fl oz warm milk
$\frac{1}{2}$ teaspoon grated nutmeg	1 oz candied peel, chopped
$\frac{1}{2}$ oz fresh yeast	1 teaspoon caraway seeds (optional)
2 oz caster sugar	1 egg yolk, beaten

Sift the flour, salt and nutmeg into a large mixing bowl. Cream the yeast with the sugar and stir into the milk with the melted butter until well blended. Pour into the flour and add the peel and caraway seeds if using. Mix well and turn out on to a floured surface. Knead well until smooth and elastic, then place the dough in a lightly oiled bowl and cover with a clean tea towel and leave to rise in a warm place until doubled in size. Knock back the dough and knead for a few minutes. Shape into 12 round buns and place on a greased baking sheet. Cover and leave in a warm place to prove for about 25 minutes until risen. Meanwhile, set oven to 425°F or Mark 7. Brush the buns lightly with beaten egg yolk and bake for 10 to 15 minutes until golden. Cool on a wire rack.

Cranberry and Orange Walnut Bread

A lovely moist loaf, unusually made with cranberries. It will keep in an airtight tin for up to a week.

8 oz flour	Finely grated rind of 1 orange
1½ teaspoons baking powder	6 fl oz orange juice
2 oz butter	1 egg, beaten
Pinch of salt	4 oz cranberries (thawed if frozen)
8 oz caster sugar	2 oz walnuts, chopped

Set oven to 350ºF or Mark 4. Grease and line a 1 lb loaf tin. Sift the flour and baking powder into a mixing bowl and rub in the butter until the mixture resembles fine breadcrumbs. Add the salt and sugar, then stir in the orange rind and juice and the egg, mixing well to combine. Gently fold in the cranberries and walnuts. Pour into the tin and bake for about 1 hour until firm. Cool in the tin for a few minutes then finish cooling on a wire rack. Wrap in foil and keep for 1 to 2 days before cutting.

Hot Cross Buns

Traditionally eaten on Good Friday.

1 lb strong white flour	2 oz granulated sugar
1 teaspoon salt	1 oz fresh yeast
1 teaspoon ground cinnamon	6 fl oz warm milk
1 teaspoon ground mixed spice	1 egg, beaten
$1/4$ teaspoon grated nutmeg	4 oz currants
2 oz butter	2 oz candied peel, chopped

2 tablespoons sugar dissolved in 2 tablespoons milk and 2 tablespoons water to glaze

Sift the flour, salt and spices into a mixing bowl. Rub in the butter. Reserve 1 teaspoon sugar and stir the rest into the flour. Cream the yeast with the reserved sugar until liquid, then stir into the warm milk and leave until frothy. Pour into the flour with the egg and mix well to a soft dough. Turn out on to a floured surface and knead well until smooth and elastic. Place a bowl, cover and leave in a warm place for one hour to rise. Then work the currants and peel into the dough, kneading well. Divide into 12 pieces and shape into buns. Place on greased baking sheets, cover and leave to prove for 25 minutes. Meanwhile, set oven to 400°F or Mark 6. Cut a cross in the top of each bun with a sharp knife, then bake for 20 minutes until golden. Two minutes before the end of the cooking time brush with the glaze and return to the oven. When cooked brush with more glaze while hot. Cool on a wire rack.

Baking Day *by William Bromley*

Soda Bread

Although Soda Bread can be found throughout the British Isles, it is most closely associated with Ireland, where it is sometimes referred to as Soda Cake. The round loaves were traditionally baked on a griddle over a peat fire.

1 lb wholemeal flour	1 teaspoon bicarbonate of soda
8 oz white flour	1 oz rolled oats (optional)
1 teaspoon salt	Approximately ½ pt buttermilk

A little beaten egg to glaze (optional)

Set oven to 425°F or Mark 7. Combine together in a bowl the flours, salt, bicarbonate of soda and rolled oats, if desired, then stir in sufficient buttermilk to make a soft dough. Turn out on a lightly floured surface and knead very lightly before shaping into a round loaf. Place on a buttered baking sheet and, using a floured knife, slash the top with a cross. Glaze with beaten egg, if desired. Bake for 20 to 30 minutes or until the loaf sounds hollow when tapped on the base. Serve warm, cut into slices with butter.

White *'special occasion'* Soda Bread can be made by replacing the wholemeal flour with white, making 1½ lb of white flour in all. Soda Bread should always be prepared as quickly as possible and handled very lightly in the process. It is not a 'keeper' so, by tradition, it should be fresh baked every morning.

Lancashire Bun Loaf

An old Lancashire recipe, which was probably first made using left over bread dough.

1½ lb strong white flour	5 fl oz warm water
½ oz salt	6 oz currants
1 sachet dried yeast	3 oz raisins
2 oz butter	3 oz sultanas
10 fl oz warm milk	2 oz candied peel, chopped

1 teaspoon mixed spice

Grease two 1 lb loaf tins. Put the flour, salt and yeast into a mixing bowl and rub in the butter. Pour in the warm milk and water and mix to a dough. Turn out on to a floured surface and knead until smooth and elastic. Put the dough into a lightly oiled bowl and cover with a clean tea towel. Leave to rise in a warm place for 1½ to 2 hours until doubled in size. Turn the dough on to a floured surface and knock back to remove all the air. Knead in the dried fruits, peel and spice and flatten to a rectangle. Roll up from the short end and put into the tins. Cover and leave to prove until doubled in size. Meanwhile, set oven to 375°F or Mark 5. When risen bake for 30 to 35 minutes. Remove from the oven and cool on a wire rack.

A Suffolk Harvest *by J. Williams*

Suffolk Buns

*Caraway seeds are the traditional flavouring ingredient for these little buns
but 3 oz of currants can be substituted if desired.*

12 oz flour	**3 oz sugar**
4 oz ground rice	**1½ oz caraway seeds**
2 teaspoons baking powder	**2 eggs, beaten**
4 oz butter	**Milk**

Set oven to 400°F or Mark 6. Mix the flour, ground rice and baking powder together.
Rub in the butter until the mixture resembles fine breadcrumbs, then stir into it the
sugar and caraway seeds, or currants if preferred. Stir in the eggs and sufficient
milk to make a smooth firm paste. Turn out on to a lightly floured surface and roll
out to 1 inch in thickness. Cut into 2 inch rounds with a cutter and place on a greased
baking sheet. Bake for 15 to 20 minutes until golden. Cool on a wire rack.

South Tyne Yeast Cake

Traditional to County Durham, this cake should be kept for at least a week before eating.

4 oz butter   4 oz sugar   1 egg, beaten   2 oz chopped mixed peel
4 oz currants   4 oz sultanas   8 oz flour
¼ oz dried yeast, dissolved in   ¼ teaspoon bicarbonate of soda,
2½ fl oz soured milk   dissolved in 2½ fl oz cold milk
1 teaspoon of sugar dissolved in 1 tablespoon warm milk to glaze

Well grease a 1 lb loaf tin. Cream the butter and sugar together in a bowl until light and fluffy, then beat in the egg and stir in the fruit and peel. Add the flour, alternately with the yeast and bicarbonate of soda mixtures and combine well. Turn out on to a lightly floured surface and knead to a smooth, soft dough. Place in the loaf tin, cover with a clean tea towel and leave in a warm place for about 30 minutes or until doubled in bulk. Set oven to 350ºF or Mark 4. Bake for 2 hours, covering the top with kitchen foil if it appears to be browning too quickly. Turn out of the tin, brush the top with the glaze and leave to cool on a wire rack.

Honey Loaf

The addition of honey helps to give this tea bread its distinctive flavour.

12 oz self-raising flour	**4 oz soft brown sugar**
1 teaspoon salt	**6 oz clear honey**
3 teaspoons mixed spice	**¼ pt milk**
2 oz candied peel, finely chopped	**1 oz lump sugar for topping**

Set oven to 350ºF or Mark 4. Grease and line a 2 lb loaf tin. Sift together into a mixing bowl the flour, salt and spice and mix in the peel and sugar. Add the honey and milk and blend together to form a smooth, stiff dough. Put into the tin, crush the lump sugar into pieces and sprinkle over the top of the loaf. Bake for 1¼ hours until brown and a skewer inserted comes out clean. Turn out and cool on a wire rack. Serve sliced and spread with butter.

Dorset Wiggs

These rich, spiced buns are traditionally served at breakfast time.

1 lb strong white flour	2 oz butter
Pinch each of ground cloves, mace and nutmeg	2 oz caster sugar
1 teaspoon caraway seeds (optional)	$\frac{1}{2}$ oz fresh yeast
	$\frac{1}{2}$ pt milk, warmed
	1 medium egg

Put the flour and spices and the caraway seeds if desired, into a large bowl. Rub in the butter and stir in the sugar. Mix the yeast to a smooth cream with a little of the warm milk. Add the yeast mixture, the egg and enough of the remaining milk to the dry ingredients to make a soft, elastic dough. Cover with a clean tea towel and leave to rise in a warm place for approximately 1½ hours until doubled in size. Shape into 6 large flat buns, put on to floured baking trays and leave to rise again for 20 minutes. Meanwhile, set oven to 400ºF or Mark 6. Bake for approximately 25 minutes until pale golden. Transfer to a wire rack to cool and serve cold, sliced and buttered.

A Dorset Dairy Farm *by Walter Tyndale*

Granary Bread

Granary flour is a proprietary mix and has a delicious malted flavour. It can be bought in Health Food shops.

1½ lb granary flour　　**1 sachet dried yeast**
1 teaspoon salt　　**14 fl oz water**
1 tablespoon vegetable oil

Put the dry ingredients into a mixing bowl, add the water and oil and mix. Gather the mixture into a ball and turn out on to a floured surface. Knead for 10 minutes until the dough is smooth and elastic. If the dough is too sticky add a little more flour, or if too dry add a little more water. Put the dough into a lightly oiled bowl and cover with a clean tea towel. Leave to rise in a warm place for 1 to 2 hours until doubled in size. Turn the dough out on to a floured surface and knock back, using the knuckles to remove all the air. Flatten out into a rectangle and roll up from underneath. Cover and leave to rise in a warm place until doubled in size. Meanwhile, set oven to 450°F or Mark 8. Bake for 15 minutes, then reduce the oven temperature to 400°F or Mark 6 and bake for another 20 to 30 minutes until cooked through. Check by removing the loaf from the tin and tap the bottom; if it sounds hollow the bread is cooked; if not, return to the oven for another 5 minutes. Turn out on to a wire rack to cool.

Victorian Dough Cake

Yeast was used as a raising agent for cakes well into the 18th century.
This Victorian recipe produces a fruit cake with a solid texture.

10 oz strong white flour	4 oz raisins
3 oz butter	4 oz sultanas
1 oz fresh yeast	3 oz dark soft brown sugar
2 oz ground rice	5 fl oz warm milk

2 eggs, beaten

Grease and line a 7 inch round cake tin. Sift the flour and sugar into a large mixing bowl and rub in the butter and yeast. Stir in the ground rice and dried fruits. Pour in the milk and beaten eggs and knead together well to form a dough. Place in the cake tin, cover with a clean tea towel and leave to rise in a warm place for 45 minutes. Meanwhile, set oven to 400°F or Mark 6. Bake for 1 hour and test that a skewer inserted comes out clean. Cool in the tin for a few minutes, then turn out and cool on a wire rack. Best eaten fresh.

An Old Surrey Corner, Witley *by Sutton Palmer*

Teacakes

Teacakes served warm, on their own or buttered, or toasted and buttered are a traditional English tea time delight.

8 oz flour	1 oz sultanas
Pinch of salt	¼ pint milk and single cream
½ oz butter	½ oz fresh yeast
1 oz sugar	1 egg, beaten

1 teaspoon of sugar dissolved in 1 tablespoon warm milk to glaze

Mix the flour and salt together in a bowl and then rub in the butter. Add the sugar and sultanas. Warm the milk and cream mixed together and stir in the yeast. When it is frothy stir into the flour mixture, then add the egg. Mix to a smooth, soft dough, then cover and leave to rise in a warm place for about 30 minutes. Set oven to 450ºF or Mark 8. Turn out on to a lightly floured surface and knead until smooth, then divide into 3 or 4 pieces and form into flat round 'cakes'. Place on a lightly greased baking tray, and leave to rise in a warm place for about 10 minutes. Bake for 10 to 12 minutes. When cooked, remove from the oven and glaze the teacakes while hot. Transfer to a wire tray to cool.

Fadge

This potato bread comes from Ireland.

8 oz potatoes, peeled   **1 oz butter, melted**
½ teaspoon salt   **2 oz flour**

Boil the potatoes until just cooked, then drain and mash until smooth and free from lumps. Add the salt and melted butter, then add the flour and mix to form a dough. Turn out on to a floured surface and roll or pat out the dough to ¼ inch thickness. Cut into rounds with a 3 inch cutter and cook on an ungreased hot griddle or heavy frying pan until browned on both sides. Serve hot with plenty of butter.

Milk Bread

A light, soft textured loaf.

3 lb strong white flour	1 oz fresh yeast
4 teaspoons salt	1 teaspoon sugar
2 oz lard	¾ pt milk

½ pt water

Sieve the flour and salt into a bowl and rub in the lard. Cream the yeast and sugar in a basin. Warm the milk and water together until tepid and add to the yeast and sugar mixture. Pour the liquid into the centre of the flour mixture. Mix to form a soft dough, turn out on to a lightly floured surface and knead for 5 minutes. Place in a bowl, cover with a clean tea towel and leave in a warm place to prove for one hour. Grease two 2 lb loaf tins. Knock back the dough and knead lightly. Divide the dough between the tins or shape into loaves and put on to a greased baking tray(s). Prove for thirty minutes. Meanwhile, set oven to 425°F or Mark 7. Bake for 10 minutes then reduce the heat to 400°F or Mark 6 for 30 minutes. Remove the loaves from the tins, turn over and bake for a further 10 minutes to brown the crust. Transfer to a wire rack to cool. Serve sliced, with butter and jam.

Chester Buns

A yeast-based bun containing condensed milk.

1 lb strong white flour	**1 teaspoon sugar**
2 level teaspoons salt	**5 dessertspoons warm milk**
2 oz butter	**1 egg, beaten**
½ oz fresh yeast	**5 fl oz condensed milk**

2 teaspoons sugar dissolved in a little warm water to glaze

Sift the flour and salt together into a bowl, then rub in the butter. Cream the yeast together with the sugar and warm milk. Allow to stand for 5 minutes or until frothy. Make a well in the flour mixture and stir in the beaten egg, condensed milk and the yeast mixture. Blend to a smooth dough, then turn out on to a lightly floured surface and knead until elastic; about 10 minutes. Form into a ball, place in a bowl, cover with a clean tea towel and put in a warm place until the dough has roughly doubled in size. Turn out and knead again lightly, then form into 12 to 14 smooth round buns. Set on a large well greased baking sheet, cover with a tea towel and leave to prove for 20 minutes. Meanwhile, set oven to 425ºF or Mark 7. Bake the buns for 15 to 20 minutes or until golden. Brush with sugar-water to glaze while still warm, then cool on a wire rack. Serve split in half and buttered.

The Falcon Inn, Chester *by E. Harrison Compton*

Crumpets

Homemade crumpets are much lighter than commercial versions.

8 oz flour
8 oz strong white flour
2 teaspoons salt
1 pint milk and water, mixed

2 tablespoons vegetable oil
1 tablespoon caster sugar
½ oz fresh yeast
½ teaspoon bicarbonate of soda

4 fl oz warm water

Sift the flours and salt into a large mixing bowl and make a well in the centre. In a pan, gently heat together the mixed milk and water, the oil and sugar until warm but not hot. Mix the yeast with a quarter of this liquid. Pour this into the well, followed by the remaining liquid and beat well until smooth and elastic; about 5 minutes. Cover with a clean tea towel and leave to rise in a warm place for about 1½ hours until frothy and about to collapse. Dissolve the bicarbonate of soda in the warm water and stir into the batter. Cover and leave to rise for 30 minutes. Place metal rings or cutters on a lightly greased griddle or heavy frying pan and warm over a medium heat. Pour the batter into the rings, about ½ inch deep and cook gently for 5 to 6 minutes. The tops should be dry with a mass of tiny holes. Remove the rings or cutters and turn the crumpets over. Cook for 2 minutes until golden brown. Repeat with the rest of the batter. Toast on both sides, spread liberally with butter and allow to saturate the warm crumpet.

Whitsun Cake

A rich speciality from Lincolnshire. It was specially made for the Whitsuntide festivities.

12 oz strong white flour	**4 oz melted butter**
Pinch of salt	**8 oz raisins**
3 oz butter	**8 oz soft brown sugar**
½ oz fresh yeast	**Pinch of grated nutmeg**
5 fl oz warm milk	**Pinch of ground cinnamon**

1 egg, separated

Set oven to 400°F or Mark 6. Grease an 8 inch round cake tin. Sift the flour and salt into a large mixing bowl and rub in the cold butter. Crumble the yeast into the warm milk and leave until frothy, then add to the flour with 3 oz of the melted butter. Knead to a soft dough, then cover with a clean tea towel and leave to rise for 45 minutes. Meanwhile mix the raisins, sugar and spices with the remaining melted butter in a pan and simmer gently for 10 minutes. Leave to cool then beat in the egg yolk. Divide the dough into 4 pieces and roll out on a floured surface to fit the base of the cake tin. Place one round of dough in the tin and top with a third of the raisin mixture. Repeat twice more and top with the remaining dough. Seal the edges of each round of dough firmly with a little egg white. Bake for 45 minutes, then brush with the rest of the egg white and return to the oven for another 10 minutes. Turn out on to a wire rack to cool. Keep in an airtight tin for 2 days before eating to allow the filling to flavour the dough layers.

Anne Hathaway's Cottage, Shottery *by W. W. Quartremain*

Oat Bread

This sweet bread, which is an old Warwickshire recipe, contains no yeast but uses baking powder as its raising agent. It develops a cake-like consistency when baked and is delicious served spread with butter.

¾ pt milk	4 teaspoons baking powder
4 oz porridge or rolled oats	6 oz caster sugar
12 oz flour	1 egg, beaten
1 teaspoon salt	½ oz butter, melted

Scald the milk by pouring into a saucepan and heating gently until bubbles begin to appear round the rim of the milk. Then pour over the oats in a bowl, stir lightly and leave to cool. In another bowl, sieve together the flour, salt and baking powder, then stir in the sugar. Beat in the egg and melted butter, then stir in the oat mixture and combine well; it will be the consistency of very thick porridge. Turn into a well buttered 2 lb loaf tin and leave to stand for 15 to 20 minutes. Meanwhile, set oven to 350ºF or Mark 4. When proved, bake for 1½ hours. After about ½ hour cover the top with a piece of *very* lightly buttered kitchen foil to prevent the top from browning too much. Turn out on to a wire rack to cool. Serve thickly sliced and spread with plenty of butter. Oat Bread is not a long-term keeper.

Aberdeen Buttery Rowies

Similar to French croissants but flatter and saltier, rowies are served warm for breakfast.

1 lb strong white flour   **10 fl oz warm milk and water, mixed**
1 oz fresh yeast   **1 teaspoon salt**
1 teaspoon caster sugar   **6 oz butter**   **6 oz lard**

Dissolve the sugar in half the milk and water and crumble in the yeast. Stir and leave until frothy; 5 to 10 minutes. Sift the flour and salt into a mixing bowl and gradually add the yeast mixture and remaining liquid to form a dough. Turn out on to a floured surface and knead for about 10 minutes until the dough is smooth and elastic. Put into a lightly oiled bowl and cover with a clean tea towel. Leave in a warm place until doubled in size. Knock back the dough and knead again for a few minutes. Roll out to a rectangle about ½ inch thick. Spread a third of the butter and a third of the lard on the top two-thirds of the dough. Fold up the bottom third and fold down the top third of dough and seal the edges. Turn the dough round and roll out again. Leave in a cool place for 10 minutes, then repeat the process twice more with the remaining fat, resting for 10 minutes each time. Finally roll out the dough about ½ inch thick and divide into 16 pieces. Shape each piece into an oval, pressing the dough out with the hands and place on greased, floured baking sheets. Cover and leave in a warm place to prove for 30 minutes. Meanwhile, set oven to 425°F or Mark 7. Bake for 15 minutes until golden brown. Serve warm with butter.